The Beautiful Northwest

A Sunset Pictorial

The Beautiful

A Sunset Pictorial

Northwest

By the Editors of Sunset Books and Sunset Magazine

Book Editor: Dorothy Krell
Design: Joseph S. Seney and William Gibson

LANE PUBLISHING CO.
MENLO PARK, CALIFORNIA

MARY RANDLETT

Front cover: Mount Adams, Washington, with aspen trees. Back cover: Lower South Falls, Silver Falls State Park, Oregon. Photographs by Russell Lamb.

Third Printing June 1980
Second Edition. Copyright © 1977, 1970 by Lane Publishing Company, Menlo Park, California.
Library of Congress No. 77-78147.
ISBN 0-376-05053-5.
Lithographed in the United States.

Editor, Sunset Books: David E. Clark

CONTENTS

The Beautiful Northwest

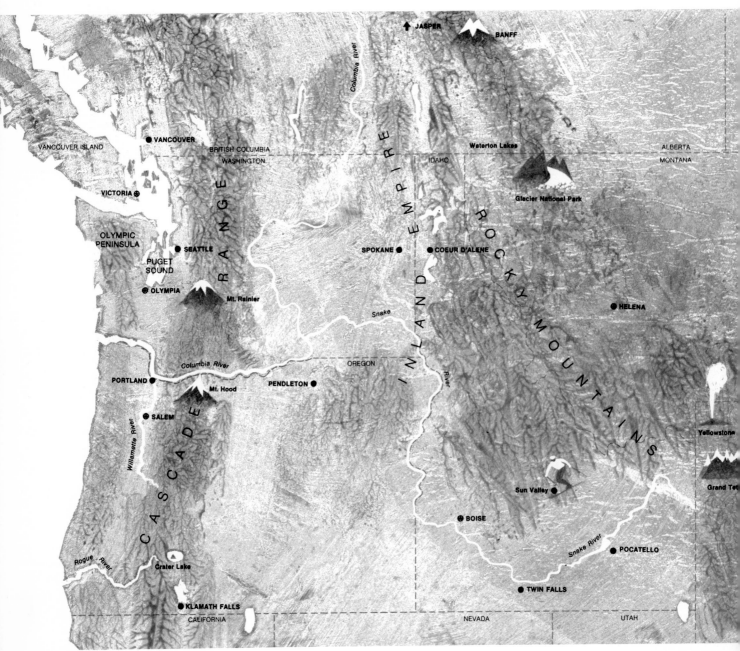

In the vast region touched on the west by the Pacific Ocean, on the south by the California and Nevada boundaries, on the east by the Rocky Mountains, and on the north by the Canadian border lies a land of almost unbelievable beauty and diversity. This is a majestic country, much of it rugged and almost untouched. Nature's bounty is evident everywhere. Northwesterners live and work within easy reach of untrampled mountain meadows, rivers that still run free, ocean beaches that are being preserved in their natural state, mountain wildernesses untouched by roads, open range land that stretches for seemingly endless unpeopled miles, dense forests that sweep over entire mountainsides. The Northwest is a paradise for the outdoorsman—fish and game are abundant, boatable lakes and rivers are plentiful, ski slopes are close to cities, campgrounds are scattered throughout beautiful forests and parks.

Along the western edge of this domain are flat beaches of hard-packed sand, forests that push to the sea, wind-swept bluffs and rocky promontories, quiet bays, protected inland waterways, bustling harbors, and major cities.

Separating this coastal region from a vastly different land to the east is the lofty spine of the Cascade Range, crowned by an imposing line of ice-clad volcanic peaks that begins in British Columbia and extends south into northern California. Within this magnificent mountain world lie craggy peaks and flower-strewn meadows, crisp mountain lakes and clear streams, deep gorges and high waterfalls, awe-inspiring panoramas and still forests. Highways cross the mountain mass in several places, and the mighty Columbia River slices through it; but for the most part, this is an almost untouched world of mountain splendor. Three national parks protect unique portions of the range. At the northern end is the great wilderness of the North Cascades National Park. In the center of the range, the greatest single-peak glacial system in the United States outside of Alaska radiates from the summit and slopes of Mount Rainier in Mount Rainier National Park. At the Oregon end, unbelievably blue Crater Lake fills the cone of a collapsed volcano in Crater Lake National Park.

The moisture-laden clouds from the Pacific drop most of their rainfall on the western side of the great barrier formed by the Cascade Range. Rainfalls of up to 200 inches per year have occurred in the rain forests of the Olympic Peninsula. Forests west of the Cascade crest are mostly Douglas fir. On the eastern slopes, Ponderosa pine predominates and the forests become more open with the trees growing in scattered stands separated by green meadows. Rolling foothills cradle river valleys where fruit orchards are a frothy mass of blossoms in the spring. The country opens up to many miles of grazing land. Mountain peaks seem closer, and alpine lakes are within a few miles of the highway that follows the eastern foothills.

East of this gentle foothill country lie the fantastic geological, archeological, and man-made wonders of the Columbia Basin, where great rivers have etched spectacular canyons into a landscape formed by lava and ice flows millions of years ago. In the heart of this great region, Grand Coulee Dam stands astride the Columbia River, an awesome monument to man's engineering ability and ingenuity in turning a million-acre desert wasteland into productive farm land.

Rich agricultural lands blanket the vast Inland Empire along the Washington-Idaho border. At the southern end are the golden wheat fields of the Palouse country. The high plateau country of eastern Oregon is broken in the north by the rolling terrain of the Blue Mountains and the more precipitous Wallowa Mountains, and far to the south, lonely Steens Mountain rises from sparsely settled desert.

Mountain ranges crisscross the northern two-thirds of Idaho, and great wilderness areas spread over the central portion of the state. Idaho's Panhandle country is a land of rushing, snow-fed rivers, many tiny lakes and a number of large ones. Most of Idaho is in the Snake River watershed, which in turn is part of the Columbia watershed. The Snake rises in the Rocky Mountains in Yellowstone National Park and flows for some one thousand miles through southern Idaho. It forms more than half of the Idaho-Oregon boundary, flowing through the deepest gorge on the North American continent before it shoots northward into Washington to join the Columbia near Pasco.

Before the explorers and the settlers came, many tribes of Indians roamed the lands west of the Rocky Mountains. Today cities bear their names and the names of many of their chiefs. Seattle was named for Chief Sealth, who befriended early pioneers. Spokane, Yakima, Shoshone, Siletz, and innumerable other towns and cities were named for Indian tribes. Rivers, mountain tops, national forests, street names, and ferry boats carry names that are reminders of the Northwest's Indian heritage.

The first outsiders to approach this country were the seafarers of the sixteenth and seventeenth centuries who sailed along the western shores in search of the fabled Northwest Passage. Next came the fur traders, who developed a profitable fur trade with the Indians of the coastal villages. Captain James Cook of England arrived in 1778 and put in at Nootka on what is now Vancouver Island. In 1792, Captain Robert Gray, an American in the service of a New England mercantile firm, sailed into the mouth of the Columbia River and named the river after his ship.

The first Americans to reach the mouth of the river from the east were the members of the Lewis and Clark Expedition who followed the route westward in 1805 and camped near the river's mouth in the winter of 1805-06. The mighty Columbia was a major influence in the development of the Northwest. Fur traders and trappers followed the explorers. In 1811, John Jacob Astor set up the Pacific Fur Company trading post of Astoria near the river's mouth. Other American and English fur traders rushed to set up trading posts along the Columbia. Then came the missionaries and the settlers, who used the great waterway to make their way to the other side of the mountain barrier that lay between them and their dreams of a great new life.

The Willamette and other western waterways soon began to play a role in the Northwest's history. The great Willamette River was to its valley what the Mississippi and Ohio Rivers were to the middle United States. From the time the first trappers began to headquarter up the river in 1811 until the railroads were completed in 1871, the Willamette was the one and only carrier of commerce in the valley. Towns grew up around its ferries, shipping points, and mill sites. Oregon City, the first city to form on the Willamette, was the first incorporated town west of the Mississippi. By 1845, Portland was a sixteen-block river town on the west bank. In 1848, the Oregon Territory was established encompassing the present states of Oregon, Washington, Idaho, and parts of Montana and Wyoming—the "Beautiful Northwest" of this book.

The settlers of Oregon soon began to move northward across the Columbia. Cities began to take shape around Puget Sound. By 1851, Olympia was a thriving village, Port Townsend was a growing seaport at the entrance to Puget Sound, and Alki Point was settled in what is now part of Seattle. In 1853, the Territory of Washington was formed covering the present state of Washington, western Montana, and northern Idaho. The Oregon portion was granted statehood in 1859.

Seven years after the Territory of Washington was formed, gold was discovered in what is now part of Idaho's Clearwater County. The great influx of miners and settlers that soon populated that region led to the creation of a separate Territory of Idaho in 1863. As the economy and population of the Northwest grew, and as rail and telegraph communication with the eastern portion of the country became a fact, other moves for statehood followed. Washington became a state in 1889, and Idaho, after five boundary changes from Oregon Territory days, entered the Union in 1890.

The dynamic growth of the Northwest begun by its hardy pioneers continues today. Lumbering, a mainstay of the economy in early days, is still a leading industry, now developed under careful conservation practices to protect this important resource. Mining continues to be important. Agriculture is highly developed. Where Lewis and Clark struggled to transport boats and men past the Columbia River rapids, huge dams now supply billions of kilowatt-hours of electricity annually and navigation locks enable barges to reach cities far upriver. Fishing is important commercially along the Northwest's coast.

The diverse attractions of the Northwest continue to bring new residents and visitors. Today they find it easier to cross the barriers—the mountains and rivers, arid desert and dense forest—and to reach every fascinating corner of this great section of the country. Yet despite this easier accessibility, much of the magnificent scenery remains little changed from that viewed by the earliest arrivals. Hopefully this beauty will remain far into the future.

THE NORTHWEST

COAST

The Northwest coast is a land of contrasts. At times it is wild and wave-battered, at other times quiet and restful. All along its length there is variety: long, sandy beaches, steep headlands, lush pastures, rocky coves, patches of deep forest. Industry is mostly lumbering and commercial fishing, but there are dairy farms and cheese factories around Tillamook, cranberry bogs and oyster beds on the North Beach Peninsula, bulb fields near Brookings. Coos Bay and Grays Harbor are busy shipping ports. Snug harbors shelter small commercial fishing boats and private and charter craft. There are resort and vacation homes, especially on the central Oregon coast and on Washington's North Beach Peninsula. But for the most part the Northwest coast remains in its natural state. Beaches for walking are tucked between dramatic bluffs and rocky headlands that offer magnificent panoramas of spectacular seascapes. Waves wash up on flat, sandy beaches or crash on rocky promontories. Here and there wildflowers bloom at the ocean's edge, and picturesque lighthouses crown lonely points. Beachcombing is at its best: rockhounds look for agates, jasper, and jade; the sculptor seeks driftwood; the naturalist studies tide pools. Anglers can choose from rock, jetty, surf, lake, stream, or deep sea fishing. This is a place for photographers, hikers, picnickers, campers, and for those who want nothing more than a few relaxing moments in beautiful, unpeopled surroundings.

PHOTOGRAPH BY MARY RANDLETT

A BEACH FOR WALKING curves along the ocean's edge near Port Orford. Below wooded bluffs, driftwood heaped ashore by winter storms weathers to a silvery gray.

JAGGED SEA STACKS rise gaunt and ghostly from the surf that rolls up on the mist-shrouded shore near Bandon on Oregon's southern coast.

THE NORTHWEST COAST   **13**

LITTLE THINGS bring special delight to those who love the ocean's shore: A sea gull takes off with a flap of wings and an irate screech when interrupted at his foraging; the horizon appears fleetingly in the view through a giant bubble of foam; a little girl and a quizzical bird share the fascination of their chance encounter.

DAVID MUENCH

A GIANT SCULPTURE, bleached by the sun and polished smooth by the elements, frames a view of beachcombers at Cape Meares. The beautiful wave-swept beaches of the Northwest's coast are rich with discoveries for photographers, artists, and collectors.

15

DON NORMARK

FROM ROCKY PERCHES above the surf, fishermen land good catches of ling cod, greenling, sculpin, and shallow-water rockfishes. Near Coos Bay (above), two saltwater ecological ranges overlap, providing anglers with more different species than almost anywhere else on the coast.

Dungeness crab

Tide pool explorer

Sun star

Goose barnacles, mussels

Giant green anemones

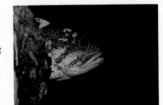

Copper rockfish

Blood star

Sea urchins

Anemones

LIFE IN THE TIDAL ZONE never ceases to fascinate its viewers whether they
be amateur tide pool explorers, students in marine biology, or scientists. It
sometimes takes perseverance to glimpse the tiny creatures that dart
from shallow pool to shadowy crevice or inch their way slowly across the surface
of a rock, but patience and a discerning eye most likely will be rewarded—perhaps
by the sight of one of the many kinds of starfish that inhabit these rocky
communities, or a cluster of spiny sea urchins or flowerlike sea anemones tucked
between camouflaging rocks, or a Dungeness crab scurrying across a sandy pool.

PHOTOGRAPHS BY JEFFERSON GONOR, STEVEN C. WILSON (TOP CENTER), BETTY RANDALL (BOTTOM LEFT)

COMMERCIAL FISHERMEN load rock
cod and shrimp at Port Orford. At right,
charter and commercial boats
fill berths at Charleston's popular
small craft harbor.

COOS BAY, bustling seaport,
is a place to watch freighters
being loaded. Their cargo is largely
forest products.

THE NORTHWEST COAST **19**

SPLASHES OF COLOR occasionally interrupt the coast's wooded bluffs, rocky shores, and wind-rippled dunes. Here and there, a weathered lighthouse stands sentry on a lonely point. In late spring, blankets of blue or yellow lupine and patches of Scotch broom brighten the landscape along with azaleas, rhododendrons, salmon pink salal, and dogwood.

RUSSELL LAMB

A FROTH OF FOAM rushes over the rocks at Boiler Bay as an enormous, wind-whipped breaker booms against the dark shore. The constant surging of the sea and occasional fierce poundings by waves like this forever shape and reshape the Northwest's beautiful coastline. There are many vantage points for wave-watching.

A STURDY LITTLE DORY takes a party of salmon fishermen seaward from Pacific City. Although the dory is traditionally associated with the codfishing on the North Atlantic's Grand Bank, salmon fishermen in the Northwest have found the nimble craft ideally suited to the rough water of the Pacific coast. Wide amidships and pointed at both ends (or slightly squared off to accommodate an outboard motor), the dories ride high on the waves. They may look top heavy, but they are the most maneuverable of all boats and the most stable of all keelless boats.

A LATE-DAY STROLL at the edge of a sparkling sea is a refreshing end to a warm summer day. Gentle waves lap at the bare feet of these two beach walkers at Short Sands State Park and sweep away the tiny tracks of birds busy at the water's edge.

HUGE MONOLITHS, *eroded into grotesque shapes by the constant surging of the sea,* *loom up offshore at Cannon Beach. Their somber silhouettes provide dramatic* *subject matter for photographers.*

25

MARY RANDLETT

A TWENTY-EIGHT-MILE SPIT
of sand in the southwestern corner
of Washington holds cranberry bogs,
a thriving oyster-growing industry,
resort towns, and some of the best
razor clam concentrations on the
Pacific coast. The North Beach
Peninsula has been a vacation
destination for Northwesterners since
1889 when Portlanders traveled by
steamboat and narrow-gauge
railroad to Seaview, Long Beach,
Ocean Park, and Nahcotta.

MARY RANDLETT

BRAVING THE ELEMENTS to take advantage
of a minus tide, a huddle of
diggers heads toward a misty surf line.

MARY RANDLETT

28

ILWACO HARBOR *lies just inside the mouth of the Columbia River at the southern end of the North Beach Peninsula. Its sheltered cove, protected on the west by tall, forested headlands, is a picturesque haven for commercial and charter boats.*

THE BATTERED HULL of the S. S. Catala rests dejectedly on the shoals of Point Brown south of Grays Harbor. The vessel's career came to a sad end on the stormy New Year's Day of 1965 when she was flooded at her moorage. During her prime, more than four decades ago, she plied the waters between Vancouver and Prince Rupert as a coastal steamer. In her later years, she served as a floating hotel during the Seattle World's Fair and as a restaurant in Long Beach, California. She fittingly ended her days back in the Northwest, where she had more recently become a floating base for salmon fishermen.

OLD OYSTER SHELLS at Willapa Bay cannery are saved for reuse as mother shells.

SHELLS ARE PUNCHED, strung on wires (left), then hung on racks in bay. Free-floating oyster larvae will attach to these shells and develop into baby oysters, called spat. Above, strung shells, ready to be placed in water.

YOUNG OYSTERS *are removed from racks after one year, then planted in beds (left above) for another three years. Harvesting (center above) is done at low tide by hand or dredge. Conveyor belt (right above) takes oysters through washing, steaming process at packing plant. Oysters here are canned or smoked. Oyster stew is specialty.*

PHOTOGRAPHS BY MARY RANDLETT

THE OLYMPIC

PENINSULA

Magnificent alpine peaks, icy glaciers, cathedral-like rain forests, and wilderness beaches come together on the Olympic Peninsula in the northwest corner of Washington. In the heart of the Peninsula, a mountain wilderness rises from deep forests to a jumble of jagged mountain peaks crowned by the glacier-draped slopes of haughty Mount Olympus. On the west side of this mountain mass, dense forests press close to wild beaches where mists drift over rocky headlands, marine life thrives in rocky tide pools, and elk, deer, raccoons, and bears leave their tracks in the hard-packed sand. Here, too, are the hemisphere's finest temperate-zone rain forests, where soft light filters down through towering firs, cedars, and hemlocks, to moss-draped maples and lush ferns and ground covers. The Olympic Highway circles the mountains on the broad, low perimeter of the Peninsula. Strung along it are villages and towns, resort communities, small businesses, and farms. Spur roads lead to fishing streams and lakes, campgrounds, the starting points of trails, and into corners of Olympic National Park which preserves the mountain interior and a narrow strip of unspoiled wilderness beach. On the east side, the resort-lined Hood Canal separates the Olympic Peninsula from the Kitsap Peninsula.

PHOTOGRAPH BY DAVID MUENCH

ON THE OCEAN SIDE of the Peninsula, a narrow, fifty-mile-long strip of Olympic National Park protects a wilderness seacoast entered by roads at only two places: for an eleven-mile stretch at the southern end, and at the Quillayute River. Here mists hover over forested headlands, birds nest on offshore islands, and tidepools are rich with marine life. Beachcombing and wildlife watching are high on the list of activities. The youngsters above are trying for razor clams on the wide sand beach near the mouth of Kaloloch Creek.

HOLE-IN-THE-WALL, north of Rialto Beach, is a low-tide passageway through a typical rocky headland between flat beaches. The best tide pools on the strip are near here.

THE OLYMPIC PENINSULA **35**

RUTH KIRK

ROOSEVELT ELK roam the coastal rain forests in winter and now and then emerge to walk along the beaches. About five thousand of these great beasts, the largest remaining herd in the nation, live in Olympic National Park. Their protection was one reason the park was established. In summer most of the elk leave the lowlands for the high meadows of the Olympic Mountains. The park is a refuge for over fifty species of wild mammals that live on the Peninsula.

A WINTER STORM on the wild coast brings a special excitement, irresistible to photographers and adventurous beachwalkers. The surf sparkles in an eerie light, and huge waves toss drift logs high and heap them effortlessly against jagged rocks.

37

*DRIFTING FOG moves softly inland
along the Peninsula's river valleys
and blankets the thick forests in chill
mist. Soon it will completely
envelop this quiet little farm alongside
the Olympic Highway near Forks.*

Sword fern with spores

Mosquito on toadstool

Bracken fern

Twisted stalk

Bunchberry dogwood

Bedstraw

Beadruby

Oxalis ground cover

IN THE MOISTURE-LADEN VALLEYS of the Hoh, Queets, and Quinault rivers, where more than 150 to 200 inches of rain fall annually, each tree and shrub and fern takes its place in the scheme of things. Huge conifers, some reaching heights of 300 feet, tower over vine maples draped with curtains of clubmosses. Fallen trees, covered with lichen and mosses and attacked from within by fungi and bacteria, become nurse logs for spruce and hemlock seedlings. Huckleberry, ferns, oxalis, vanilla leaf, bedstraw, and plants too numerous to mention here grow in shady glens on the forest floor.

PHOTOGRAPHS BY RUTH KIRK

HOH VALLEY is the most accessible of the Olympic rain forests. A twenty-mile, paved road leads into it, and a hiking trail follows the river for eighteen miles.

DAVID MUENCH

THE SUMMIT of Mount Olympus is high enough (7,976 feet) and rugged enough to be a perennial challenge to experienced climbers. Here three mountaineers have reached the mountain's top; another party approaches across glacier at right.

ATOP KLAHHANE RIDGE, a resting hiker views Port Angeles, largest town on the Olympic Peninsula and a snug harbor for fishing craft, ocean-going freighters, and the ferries that cross the Strait to Victoria.

NEAR HURRICANE RIDGE, mountain goats browse quietly, unperturbed by the nearby photographer. In the high, open country of Olympic National Park, visitors may see deer, bear, raccoon, and skunk. About 140 species of birds have been identified in a variety of habitats in the park.

DOROTHY KRELL

HURRICANE RIDGE ROAD threads through green-clad mountains to the highest alpine area in the park that can easily be reached by automobile. From sea level, the road rises to 5,200 feet in 18 miles. Trails on the ridge meander through meadows that are colorful with wildflowers in midsummer.

*EDIZ HOOK curves out from Port Angeles for three miles into the Strait of
Juan de Fuca, forming a sheltered waterway for small fishing craft.
There's good year-round salmon and bottom fishing off the spit.
From the road leading to a Coast Guard station at the end of the spit,
you can look back at the city and its protected inner harbor.*

VICTORIAN HOUSES are beautifully preserved in Port Townsend. In the 1880s, this was a key city at the gateway to Puget Sound. Elegant homes overlooked Admiralty Inlet and Juan de Fuca Strait, the town's business section thrived, and new settlers arrived with each incoming ship. Then came the financial panic of 1893. The beautiful buildings, many never occupied, were deserted, businesses closed, and new residents left the city. Today Port Townsend is a museum of Victorian architecture, and homes like these reward the visitor who makes the short side trip to the northeast tip of the Peninsula.

IN SPRING flower-strewn fields are dappled with sunlight, and trees leaf out in pale greens that contrast with distant conifer-covered mountainsides. This pastoral scene is in the northeast corner of the Peninsula, near Sequim.

FLOATING BRIDGE, photographed here from a point near South Point, connects the Olympic Peninsula with the Kitsap Peninsula. The Olympic Highway follows the wooded shore of the canal for about thirty miles. Resorts catering to fishermen line both sides of the channel, especially in the lower canal area.

PLACID WATERS make Hood Canal a favorite place for kayaking. In this view from Scenic Beach State Park on the Kitsap Peninsula, you look back across the canal to the snowy Olympic Mountains.

THE PUGET

SOUND AREA

In the protected inland sea of Puget Sound and the inlets and passageways to the north, the waterways bustle with the comings and goings of ferries, steamships, freighters, tugs, and private craft of every size and description. Around the edges of this great water world, Washington's largest cities and their rapidly growing suburbs house the major portion of the state's population. The big cities are interspersed with tranquil agricultural areas. A few minutes' drive from metropolitan centers, cows graze quietly, bulb fields stretch across the flatlands against a backdrop of snowy mountains, scenic highways cross forested mountain passes, and sandy beaches edge quiet coves. Puget Sound stretches for ninety miles from its southern tip to the Strait of Juan de Fuca. It officially ends at the entrance to the Hood Canal. However, in popular usage the Sound has come to mean most of the inland waterways to the north as well. Islands are scattered like stepping stones throughout the waters between Vancouver Island and the mainland. The San Juan group has 172 islands, and just north of them, British Columbia's Gulf Islands number more than a hundred. On summer evenings, the island shores are dotted with beach bonfires. There are clam bakes, fish suppers, picnics, boating, fishing, or here and elsewhere around this water-oriented world, just relaxing in an atmosphere of slow-paced informality.

PHOTOGRAPH BY MARY RANDLETT

MUKILTEO LIGHTHOUSE perches on the shore of Possession Sound. Across the water, the wooded slopes, sandy beaches, and sheltered coves of Whidbey Island lie just a fifteen-minute ferry ride away. On busy summer weekends, the ferry landing is crowded with a miscellany of cars, campers, bicycles, motorcycles, and foot passengers headed for the island.

BOAT OWNERS around the Sound enjoy a wonderful water world of uncounted bays, inlets, islands, and beaches. There are more private boats here in relation to population than anywhere else in the West.

DOUG WILSON

DESERTED SHORES border quiet islands around the edges of the Sound. These beachcombers on Marrowstone Island find a treasure trove of weathered driftwood.

HUGH PARADISE

ON A PROTECTED BEACH at La Conner, fishermen ready their nets for the next day's trip.

MARY RANDLETT

POULSBO is built close to the shores of Liberty Bay. Fishing boats make this their winter port.

ROBERT GUNNING

58

BEAUTIFUL GARDENS surround Washington's Capitol in Olympia. Cherry trees look like huge bouquets in April, and in summer the gardens are bright with blooming annuals. Autumn brings leaf colors that set the grounds ablaze.

MAGNOLIA BLOSSOMS drift to the ground at the edge of Sylvester Park. A statue of John Rankin Rogers, former governor, overlooks the shaded grounds, and beyond, the Old State Capitol, built in 1893, still houses some state offices.

ON A CRISP AUTUMN MORNING, the vineyards along the shores of Pickering Passage turn golden and the air is filled with the fragrance of ripening grapes. Since 1878, vintners here have grown the Island Belle grape, similar to the Concord.

TRANQUIL VALLEYS, removed from the rush of traffic, lie in the quiet reaches near the southern tip of Puget Sound. Tulips and daffodils color this field in the Puyallup Valley within sight of Rainier's snowy peak.

THE PUGET SOUND AREA   **61**

DECEPTION PASS BRIDGE spans the swirling waters of the tidal passage that separates Whidbey Island from Fidalgo Island. Each time the tide changes, water rushes beneath the bridge at a velocity of five to eight knots. Cone-shaped Pass Island, at the center of the bridge, divides the narrow channel of Canoe Pass from wider Deception Pass.

THE NARROWS BRIDGE provides a connecting link between Tacoma and the Kitsap Peninsula and is a shortcut for Seattle and Tacoma area residents heading for the Hood Canal and the northern part of the Olympic Peninsula.

ALONGSIDE ELLIOTT BAY, Seattle's downtown streets climb uphill from the waterfront. Double-deck Alaskan Way viaduct follows the shoreline at the edge of the city. To the northwest, the soaring Space Needle marks Seattle Center.

KEITH GUNNAR

THE PUGET SOUND AREA 65

A WATERFRONT EXPERIENCE is not dependent on the season. Even on chilly winter days, walkers hike sandy beaches, sailors enjoy brisk breezes, and youngsters find the usual surprises at the water's edge. On a moonlit evening, a visit to the waterfront can be spectacular as ferries silently approach the city across the sparkling water.

KEITH GUNNAR

TOM TRACY

BEAUTIFUL EVENINGS make waterfront exploring memorable. A magnificent sunset casts its glow over Shilshole marina (above). Strollers at Waterfront Park (left) take advantage of a warm, still evening. This unique urban park zigzags along Elliott Bay, opening vistas of the city and Puget Sound.

KEITH GUNNAR

A PEOPLE-ORIENTED PARK spans a freeway in downtown Seattle. Water cascades into large shallow pools designed for wading. Beyond, an intricate manmade canyon rises 32 feet high and 60 feet wide, a geometric visual echo of the skyscraper cityscape around it. Ten thousand gallons of water per minute crash down the concrete cliffs with a roar that drowns out the traffic noise from the freeway.

KEITH GUNNAR

KEITH GUNNAR

STUNNING COLOR greets the springtime visitor to the University of Washington Arboretum where beautiful plantings of rhododendrons and azaleas, roses, peonies, magnolias, and lovely flowering trees border lawns and paths.

TED SPIEGEL

BOATING WATERS in and around Seattle attract all age groups. A rented rowboat is all these boys need to enjoy an afternoon on Green Lake. A park of trees and rolling lawn borders this mile-long lake, and a bicycle path circles it.

70

A DELIGHTFUL CITY PARK occupies the grounds that held the Seattle World's Fair in 1962. The Seattle Center offers attractions in rich variety, including a performing arts center, an amusement park, museums and galleries, shops and restaurants. The graceful arches above are part of the handsome plaza of the Pacific Science Center, one'of the country's most attractive and up-to-date science museums.

FOUNTAINS, pools, and tree-shaded walkways are among Seattle Center's attractions. Fountains perform from one end of the park to the other. The shooting jets of the International Fountain (left) present a show that features music and water programmed together.

STAR BOATS SKIM CHOPPY WATERS on Lake Washington. In mid-summer, hydroplane races on the thirty-mile-long lake climax the week-long festivities of Seattle's annual Seafair.

JOSEF SCAYLEA

Checking the net

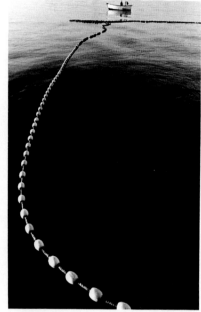

Stringing the net

Pulling the "purse"

Purse rings

A catch of salmon

Hauling in the net

THE PURSE SEINERS that operate in Puget Sound waters and the straits to the north present a picturesque sight as they pay out their nets to form the "purse" that hopefully will corral a good haul of salmon. The huge net is strung out from the stern of the purse seiner and pulled into a wide circle with the help of a power skiff. It hangs straight down, open at the bottom. Salmon encircled by the net swim in circles to avoid the obstacle but do not dive. The "pulling of the purse" occurs when brass rings attached to the bottom of the net and strung with a nylon rope are pulled tight and hauled aboard the seiner, thus drawing the bottom ends of the net together to create a "purse" open only at water level. The center of the purse is then brought aboard and the fishermen begin the process of hauling in the entire net with its catch of fish.

PHOTOGRAPHS BY TED SPIEGEL

RINGS OF WHITE circle out on an intensely blue sea as purse seiners off British Columbia coast set their nets.

75

GEORGE HUNTER

THE INNER HARBOUR, dominated by the imposing Parliament Buildings (above) and the ivy-covered Empress Hotel (below), is the heart of Victoria. The busy esplanade is crowded and colorful, with drivers hawking tours on vehicles ranging from horse-drawn tallyho to double-decker London bus. Flower-filled baskets hang from lampposts, and a floral greeting on the bank welcomes those who arrive by boat.

BUTCHART GARDENS, once a limestone quarry, is a tapestry of color spread across some 25 acres. The gardens represent many eras and regions, from the classic Italian garden with its precise topiary and sculptured fountains to the English rose garden where every variety among some 2,000 bushes is labeled.

ELIZABETH BRYAN

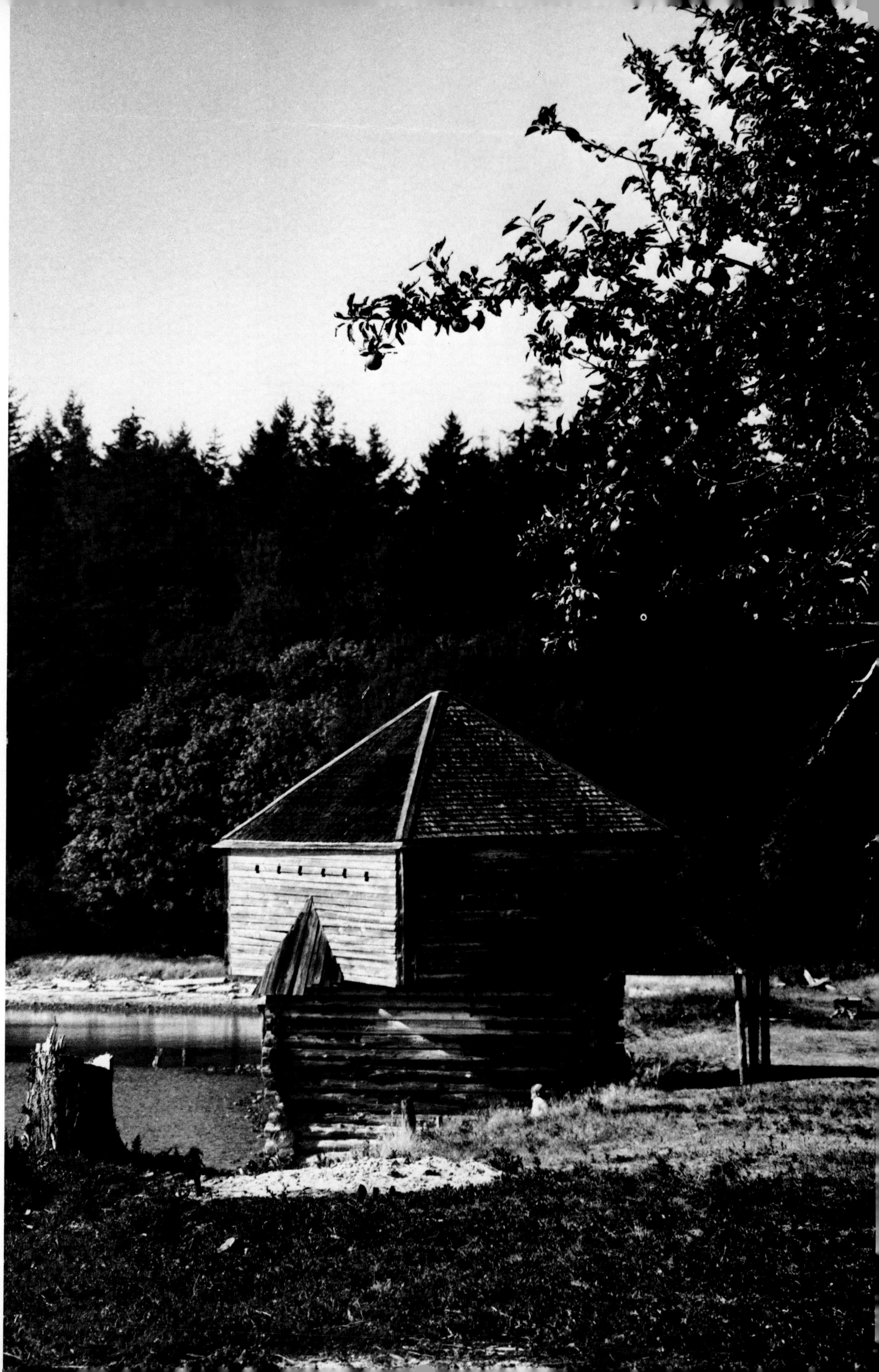

TUCKED AMONG THE MOUNTAINS that run the length of Vancouver Island, placid Cameron Lake (above) and Buttle Lake (below) mirror dark, forested shores. Between Vancouver Island and the mainland, islands are scattered like stepping stones. English Camp blockhouse (opposite) is on San Juan Island.

DOROTHY KRELL

QUEEN ELIZABETH PARK on "Little Mountain" combines a panoramic view of Vancouver with a garden that invites strolling. Paths wind through manicured grounds that cover two former rock quarries. Beyond, are the highrises of downtown Vancouver, and, across Burrand Inlet, North Vancouver and its mountain backdrop.

THE CASCADE

RANGE

Though broken by crags, bluffs, and some deep canyons, the long swell of the Cascades is generally seen as a green pedestal for majestic white volcanoes extending for 750 miles from southern British Columbia into northern California. Beginning at the north, the major cones are Baker, Glacier Peak, Rainier, St. Helens, Adams, Hood, Jefferson, the Three Sisters, Shasta, and Lassen. Viewed from certain vantage points, these giants stand out in solitary splendor, but they stand only slightly apart from a breathless company of mountain giants, all looking romantically steep and unattainable and top-heavy with ice. Mount Rainier, highest peak in the range, reaches 14,410 feet, followed closely by California's Mount Shasta, Washington's Mount Adams, and Oregon's Mount Hood. The Baker-Nooksack-Chilliwack high country athwart the Canadian border is a vast mountain subject in itself, cut off from the rest of the Cascades by the deep canyons of the Skagit River. Southeast of the upper Skagit rises the long wilderness segment of the North Cascades National Park and two national recreation areas around Ross Lake and Lake Chelan. Farther south, three other national parks—Mount Rainier, Crater Lake, and across the California border, Lassen Volcanic—preserve other segments of the majestic range. And for the entire length of the range, countless streams plunge from mountain cliffs, hundreds of lakes lie hidden in glacial valleys, summer wildflowers carpet mountain meadows, and cool evergreens shade uncrowded trails.

PHOTOGRAPH BY DAVID MUENCH

KEITH GUNNAR

MOUNT SHUKSAN looms large beyond the snowy cornices of Artists Point above the Mount Baker ski area. At right, the mountain is reflected in the mirror-smooth water of Highwood Lake.

ROBERT GUNNING

FROM AUSTIN PASS, at the top of the chair lift, skiers get this view of Mount Baker. In summer, the pass is a favorite hiking area. September and October bring berry pickers after luscious huckleberries.

THE CASCADES **89**

JOSEF SCAYLEA

THE SUMMIT ROCKS of 7,600-foot Magic Mountain in the North Cascades National Park are a challenge to serious climbers. In the distance, storm clouds gather over Eldorado Peak, center of a wilderness area that is a part of the South Unit of the park. In this section of the North Cascades near the Canadian border, 1,053 square miles of magnificent alpine scenery is conserved within the park and the Ross Lake and Lake Chelan national recreation areas.

IN LATE SUMMER, summit peaks in the Illabot Mountains of Glacier Peak Wilderness are still ice-clad, but warm summer winds and sun have developed noticeable suncups.

90 THE CASCADES

CASCADE PASS is an easily reached sampler of the North Cascades, with soaring glacier-burdened peaks, needlelike spires, and views down into forested valleys. In late July, the ridgetop meadows near the pass are blanketed with wildflowers, and you hear the deep crackling sounds of sloughing ice and tumbling avalanches when the day is warm. The peaks above, left to right, are The Triplets (7,250 feet), Cascade Peak (7,430 feet), and Johannesburg Mountain (8,065 feet).

RUTH CREEK winds through a deep, wooded, glacial valley between cloud-piercing peaks. Now and then the silence is broken by the chirp of a pika or the tumbling of a rock, and always there is a background sound of falling water, sometimes muted by distance, sometimes lost in the roar of wind.

IN THE SNOWY HEARTLAND of the North Cascades, Sahale Mountain is a
well-known climbing peak that offers a magnificent panorama of peaks and glaciers.
View is southwest across North Fork of Cascade River to Johannesburg Mountain.

94

KEITH GUNNAR

ABOVE THE CLOUDS on Chocolate Glacier, climbers look out toward distant mountain peaks from high on the slopes of 10,436-foot Glacier Peak.

MORNING MIST drifts away and the meadow glistens with dew as campers on Miner's Ridge set out for a day of walking and fishing near Image Lake.

96

MORAINE-DAMMED POND
*at the foot of Lyman Glacier
reflects Bonanza Peak, standing
high above the intervening
valley of Railroad Creek.*

MARTIN LITTON

ROBERT GUNNING

*JAGGED PEAKS of Glacier Peak Wilderness stand out against a cloud-filled
sky in this view from peak near Hidden Lake in North Cascades National Park.*

DAVE BARNES

ROCKY CRAGS tower above the
North Cascades Highway and Diablo
Lake (above). The highway traverses
national forest lands and Ross
Lake National Recreation Area to link
western Washington with Idaho. The
view at left is from Slate Peak, a
short side trip from the main highway.

DON NORMARK

UNIQUE GATEWAY to the North Cascades
from the east is the 55-mile waterway of
Lake Chelan, deep in a great trough left by a
glacier. It's a 4½-hour boat trip from Chelan
at the lower end of the lake to Stehekin in
the Lake Chelan National Recreation Area.

JOHN F. WARTH

*CRISP MOUNTAIN LAKES fill
hundreds of tiny glaciated basins
between Snoqualmie Pass and Stevens
Pass. No roads lead to them, but
they are favorite destinations of
wilderness explorers. In autumn,
the lakes take on varied
colors. Larch trees stand out against
the snow-dusted slopes around
Rune Lake (above). The still surface
of Nada Lake (left) mirrors jagged gray
slopes and a reed-grown shore.
The brilliant foliage of mountain ash
and huckleberry brightens the
shore around Gem Lake (right).*

THE CASCADES **101**

DAVID MUENCH

MAJESTIC MOUNT RAINIER dominates the view from Sunrise, and far below the White River is a twisting, silvery thread through its narrow valley. The 14,410-foot dormant volcano is mantled by 26 glaciers, more than on any other mountain in the United States outside of Alaska. Their ice covers 40 square miles of the 378 square miles that comprise Mount Rainier National Park. From here you see Emmons Glacier, one of several that originate at the summit.

CLOUDS AND MOUNTAIN TOPS stretch to the horizon in this view from the 10,000-foot level on Mount Rainier. Mount Adams to the south seems very close. Far in the distance, Mount Hood and Mount Jefferson reach into Oregon skies. For those who enjoy mountain climbing, Rainier is a worthy challenge. Some 2,400 climbers reach the summit each year after a strenuous ascent over lava, glaciers, and ice fields.

COMET FALLS, highest waterfall in Mount Rainier National Park (320 feet) is fed by melt from Van Trump Glacier on the south side of the mountain. Note tiny figures on slope at right of the falls.

PHOTOGRAPHS BY KEITH GUNNAR

FROM THE TRAILS you get a closeup look at Mount Rainier's forests and parklike meadows. Wildflowers begin to appear in mid-June as the snow recedes, and later in the summer, entire slopes are cloaked in color. Hiking is popular in the park; trails range from short nature walks to the 90-mile Wonderland Trail that encircles the mountain.

BOB & IRA SPRING

NEARLY PERFECT in its symmetry, snow-covered Mount St. Helens (right) is one of the most beautiful peaks in the Cascades. Spirit Lake, fringed with dark forests, nestles at its base and forms the nucleus of a mountain recreation area in Gifford Pinchot National Forest. From the summit of the mountain, a magnificent panorama includes the neighboring peaks of Rainier, Adams (above), and Hood.

APPLE COUNTRY begins in the Thompson Valley of British Columbia and extends down the Wenatchee and Yakima valleys of Washington and across the Columbia into Oregon's quiet Hood River valley. The Northwest's orchards produce over thirty million bushels of apples a year. In spring the valleys are a froth of snowy, fragrant blossoms. In autumn they bustle with the activity of the big harvest, and roadside stands along quiet roads are heaped with boxes of just-picked fruit.

THE CASCADES 109

RAY ATKESON

GENTLE MOUNTAINS, clear lakes, and inviting trails lie in a friendly wilderness just beyond this quiet grazing land near Bend. The Cascade Lakes Highway and roads leading from it go almost to the foot of craggy-rimmed Broken Top (above) and South Sister in the Three Sisters Wilderness. Among the more than 240 miles of trails inside the wilderness, there are easy ones and some that challenge the most capable hiker.

QUIET WATERS reflect mountain
hemlock in one of dozens of small
lakes in the roadless wilderness.
On this east side of the mountains,
access to the wilderness is easy,
and this is a popular region for fishing,
hiking, horseback riding, swimming,
and boating.

WILLIAM APLIN

DAVID MUENCH

ELK LAKE reflects the volcanic peak of South Sister. Located just outside the
wilderness area, Elk Lake is a departure point for trail trips to lakes
on the east slopes of the mountains.

111

OREGON'S COVERED BRIDGES are fast disappearing, but there are still about one hundred of them spanning streams west of the Cascades. Goodpasture Bridge (above), built in 1938, spans the McKenzie near Leaburg. Below, Fall Creek glides prettily under Pengra Bridge. It is not deterioration that is bringing about the replacement of the covered bridges. The sheltered wooden spans hold up well, but traffic today is far heavier than was foreseen when they were built during the 1920's and 1930's.

MCKENZIE RIVER RAPIDS call for special boating skill. River guides know the river and its rewarding fishing spots. Their boats are specially built, with upturned ends and shallow draft.

DIAMOND LAKE is quiet and deserted on a wintry day. The vacationers have left its resorts and campgrounds. The storm clouds that have dropped a dusting of snow on the mountain peaks across the lake soon will bring the first snowfall of the season to the empty shore.

WIZARD ISLAND rises from the incredibly blue waters of Crater Lake, formed when Mount Mazama, a 12,000-foot volcanic peak, collapsed almost 6,600 years ago. Only six lakes in the world are deeper.

DAVID MUENCH

OREGON'S
RIVER

WESTERN VALLEYS

From the snowy crest of the Cascade Range and from the lower slopes of the Coast Range, gentle rivers, meandering streams, and some rushing torrents thread their way through narrow canyons, rural valleys, towns and cities on their way to the sea. Three major river valleys and a number of small ones lie west of the Cascades in Oregon. The Rogue and the Umpqua originate in the Cascade snow packs, then cut through the Coast Range to the Pacific. Other rivers—notably the Coquille, Smith, Siuslaw, Alsea, Yaquina, Siletz, Nestucca, and Nehalem—begin in the Coast Range and flow to the ocean. South of Eugene, the mighty Willamette begins in two forks: a fast, clear-water stream out of the Cascades and a slow, muddy one out of the Coast Range. It flows north, joined shortly by the also-mighty McKenzie, rushing down out of the Cascades. At Eugene it begins a winding course through the 125-mile-long, agriculturally rich Willamette Valley to Portland, where it enters the West's greatest river, the Columbia. On its way north, the Willamette's volume is increased with waters from many more Cascade and Coast Range rivers and creeks. From the Cascades come the Calapooya, the Santiam, the Pudding, the Molalla, the Clackamas; from the Coast Range, the Long Tom, Mary's River, the Luckiamute, the Yamhill, the Tualatin. Oregon's largest city, Portland, and its capital city, Salem, lie in the valley of the Willamette. Other towns and cities, many historic sites and buildings, delightful parks and roadside rests, border this and other rivers, and many lovely tree-shaded banks provide scenic campsites and quiet spots for picnicking and fishing.

PHOTOGRAPH BY RAY ATKESON

GEORGE KNIGHT

PEAR ORCHARDS stretch for miles
across the Rogue River valley near
Medford. At the edges of the valley,
gentle foothills rise to the
timbered slopes of the Siskiyous.

HISTORIC JACKSONVILLE grew when gold was discovered in nearby Rich Gulch in 1851. The town has deteriorated surprisingly little in the years since. Quiet streets like the one below invite strolling. Many of the town's 19th century wood and brick buildings have been restored. The United States Hotel (above) hosted President Rutherford B. Hayes and his party in 1880; now it houses a local bank.

A TOWN FOR PLAYGOERS, Ashland keeps audiences entertained from mid-February through September. From its beginning as a three-day event in 1935, Ashland's famed Oregon Shakespearean Festival has grown to a nationally recognized event. To set the mood before summer performances in the open-air Elizabethan Theatre (below), costumed dancers entertain in the theater gardens.

A PEACEFUL RURAL VALLEY lies south of Grants Pass along the Applegate River that winds through the foothills of the Siskiyous. In spring, pear, peach, cherry, apricot, and apple trees bloom, and the fields are splashed with wildflowers.

A FAMED FISHING RIVER, the Rogue has always been a challenge to anglers. Its legendary runs of steelhead and salmon rate most of the enthusiasm, but the Rogue and its main tributaries offer good rainbow trout fishing as well.

122

GRAZING LAND north of Grants Pass is pleasant auto exploring country. Back roads lead to tranquil scenery and pleasant picnic sites. For the more venturesome, Grants Pass is the departure point for hiking trips in the roadless country along the Rogue River.

WATER ADVENTURES ON THE ROGUE take several forms. Most unforgettable ride of them all is the white-water trip from Grants Pass to the ocean (above). River guides take passengers through this wild stretch in specially built boats. Jet-propelled boats (left) go from Grants Pass to spectacular Hellgate Canyon. At the lower end of the river, passenger-carrying mail boats (below) climb the riffles daily from Gold Beach on the coast to Agness, 32 thrilling miles upstream.

OREGON'S WESTERN RIVER VALLEYS **125**

THE MOODS OF A RIVER are varied and changeable. The Coquille is quiet here as it glides smoothly between mossy banks and swirls around softly sculpted boulders. Now and then it cascades gently down shallow falls, and here and there its banks are brightened by a tuft of fresh green grass or a jaunty clump of wildflowers.

PHOTOGRAPHS BY DAVID MUENCH

MORLEY BAER

THE COQUILLE AND THE UMPQUA were important waterways in early days.
In the 1850's tall-masted schooners carried gold miners and supplies from
San Francisco along the coast and then up the Umpqua (right) to Scottsburg. Clumsy
old stern-wheelers plied the Coquille (above) long before the construction of the
modern highway, and one of the first lumber mills in Camas Valley was built on
the river's headwaters. Now both placid rivers are edged by roads, and families
picnic along their shores beneath maple and myrtle trees.

RAY ATKESON

DON NORMARK

TYPICALLY ORNATE WOODWORK, known as gingerbread or carpenter's Gothic, embellishes nineteenth-century buildings in Eugene. The Willamette Valley, which begins just south of here, probably harbors more pre-1900 structures than any other area of comparable size in the West. These in Eugene are typical. Deady Hall (above) on the University of Oregon campus, was completed in 1876 to house the first classrooms of the university. The other buildings shown here are all privately occupied residences.

AT HARVEST TIME, the gentle rolling hills that border the Willamette and Tualatin river valleys turn golden brown. At other times during the year, they are billowy green. Despite the rapid growth of these areas, the valleys remain essentially rural.

FILBERT ORCHARDS pattern many acres in the northern part of the Willamette Valley, producing almost ninety percent of the nation's crop.

OREGON'S WESTERN RIVER VALLEYS   133

OREGON'S CAPITOL shows the state's early history in its theme. A 24-foot statue of a bearded, ax-wielding pioneer tops its cylindrical dome. Marble sculptures on each side of the entrance depict the Lewis and Clark Expedition and the covered wagons that pioneered the Oregon Trail. Inside the building, panels around the rotunda picture the original wagon trails along the Willamette and Columbia rivers. Those who climb the stairway to the capitol dome are rewarded with a fine view of Salem, Mount Hood, and the Cascades.

LOWER SOUTH FALLS tumbles 93 feet over a steep precipice in Silver Falls State Park. This is one of 14 waterfalls in the lovely wooded canyons of the park.

OREGON'S WESTERN RIVER VALLEYS   **139**

A RIVER PARKWAY 225 miles long, the Willamette winds through Oregon's most populous region. It offers white water, lazy stretches, sun-warmed backwaters, and lower reaches deep enough and wide enough for ocean-going freighters. The paddlers above attempt rapids at Springfield. On the Portland section of the river, the boys test their maneuvering skill in a rubber raft.

BELOW WILLAMETTE FALLS, fishermen pursue a run of Chinook salmon. In the early 1960s, the Willamette was so heavily polluted that salmon runs were almost nonexistent. Since then, cities, towns, and the state have cooperated in a successful cleanup of the river, and the salmon have returned to spawn.

WINDING THROUGH PORTLAND, the broad Willamette River divides the city. Ten auto bridges span the waterway. West of the river, lovely residential areas overlook the tall buildings of downtown. Higher on the hills, in a unique 5,000-acre park system, deer wander freely in forests of Douglas fir, western red cedar, and hemlock.

WATERFALLS crash over concrete walls, drowning out city noises and making the Forecourt Fountain a pleasant retreat in the midst of downtown bustle. People picnic, read, and meditate on concrete perches on the fountain or grassy areas nearby. Quiet pools above and below the falls invite foot-dangling or wading.

ROSES ARE EVERYWHERE in Portland. At right, they bloom beneath a statue of Theodore Roosevelt in a downtown Park Block. The handsome modern building in the background houses the Oregon Historical Society and its fine historical exhibits. Below, roses are an important landscaping element in the sunken garden of a downtown office building.

RAY ATKESON

AN INDIAN SUMMER HAZE softens the light that filters through giant elm trees in one of Portland's downtown Park Blocks. Three sets of Park Blocks, the largest set running for fourteen consecutive blocks, are wisely kept as landscaped open space in the heart of the city.

GEORGE KNIGHT

THE PORTLAND OF THE PAST has been preserved and enhanced in these two former homes now open to the public. The impressive Pittock Mansion (above) overlooks the city from a wooded hilltop west of the Willamette. In a pastoral setting on quiet Sauvie Island, restored Bybee-Howell House (below) reflects life in the Oregon country on the eve of statehood when territorial settlers lived an isolated, self-contained life here. Behind the house, apple trees dominate an orchard planted with 160 varieties of fruit trees found in early Oregon orchards.

RUSSELL LAMB

146

DON NORMARK

GEORGE KNIGHT

BISHOP'S HOUSE (left), reportedly once just that, later became a Chinese speakeasy, now houses offices. One-time commercial center of the city was the area around Skidmore Fountain (above). This 1888 gift to the city, now restored after years of neglect, was a favorite meeting place for two generations of Portlanders.

GARDENS FOR STROLLING are easy to find in Portland. Rhododendrons and azaleas burst into colorful bloom in April and May in the test gardens of the American Rhododendron Society in Crystal Spring Lake Park (above). Tranquility greets the visitor to the Japanese Garden in Washington Park (below) where five classic garden forms spread over 5 ½ hillside acres.

A PORTLAND SHOWPLACE, the International Rose Test Gardens step down a terraced slope overlooking the city. The roses bloom from late May into fall. They are at their best in early June when Portland holds its famed week-long Rose Festival.

THE COLUMBIA

RIVER

From its origin in Columbia Lake, high in the British Columbia Rocky Mountains, the mighty Columbia travels more than 1,200 miles on its way to the Pacific. For a time the river flows north, looping around the Selkirk Mountains. Then it heads abruptly south through the wide trough between the Selkirks and the Monashees. Below the Canadian border, the Columbia is tamed behind the enormous concrete structure of Coulee Dam, and its waters are diverted to irrigate a million-acre tract of former desert in the vast Columbia Basin. Farther downstream, other dams slow the river, tapping its strength for hydroelectric power and irrigation. The river travels through orchard lands, quiet farm valleys, wheat fields and range land, forested mountains, and arid plateau country, and is the only river that has managed to slice through the barrier of the Cascade Range. Major tributaries flow into it—Washington's Pend Oreille, Spokane, Okanogan, Wenatchee, Yakima; its largest tributary, the Snake; Oregon's John Day and Willamette—to drain more than 259,000 square miles in Canada and seven western states. For much of its length, the Columbia is bordered by major highways. Side roads lead to feathery waterfalls that cascade over nearly vertical cliffs, view points that overlook magnificent river vistas, dry river channels, fossil caves, exposed ancient lava flows, streams and lakes to fish, and an uncrowded countryside to explore.

PHOTOGRAPH BY RAY ATKESON

OFF THE NORTH JETTY, ships bounce like bathtub toys as they cross the Columbia River Bar. For over a century, the Bar has brought grief to sailors. Some two hundred major shipwrecks are on record for this section of the coast.

MARY RANDLETT

ATOP WAVE-BATTERED BLUFFS, two picturesque lighthouses mark the entrance to the Columbia. North Head Light (left) crowns a windswept cliff on the ocean side of a rugged headland. On the river side, Canby Light (below) flashes its warning from the forested shore of Cape Disappointment.

GEORGE KNIGHT

ASTORIA'S FISHING FLEET anchors at the base of a wooded hill dotted with homes that overlook the busy Columbia. Astoria Column (right) crowns 700-foot Coxcomb Hill. The frieze that spirals around it depicts major events in the town's history.

154

SPANNING THE COLUMBIA at Astoria, a 4-mile-long toll bridge links the Oregon and Washington shores. The structure rises high over the water on the approach from Astoria, then continues at water level for most of its length.

VISIBLE FOR MILES along the Columbia, Beacon Rock is a towering giant that rises 848 feet above the Columbia Gorge. A trail, much of it consisting of narrow bridges, ramps, and steps, zigzags up the sheer escarpment.

FROM THE TOP of the rock, the panorama is magnificent. In this view eastward, the river disappears between folds of forested hills.

HIGH ABOVE THE RIVER, a 22-mile scenic stretch of the old Columbia River Highway overlooks the Columbia Gorge. You see weather in the making as you look east up the windswept, cloud-shadowed waterway toward Crown Point and its Vista House. Far below, a modern freeway speeds travelers through the Gorge at water level past Rooster Rock Park, popular day-trip destination for Portlanders.

DONALD MCKEEHEN

THE RIVER CUTS DEEP into a treeless rugged plateau near Vantage. The long, slim line of the Vantage Bridge spans the Columbia between tawny bluffs just north of Wanapum Dam, carrying the traffic of Interstate 90, major east-west route across central Washington.

AUTUMN GOLD colors the trees in the long valley of the Okanogan River. The highway that threads through the entire length of the valley from the Columbia to Shuswap Lake in British Columbia follows the route of the Cariboo Trail, trod in turn by Indians, fur brigades, and gold seekers. On the Canadian side of the border, the valley's name changes to Okanagan.

WILLIAM CARTER

THE COLUMBIA RIVER   **165**

DAVID MUENCH

FROM THE TOP of Grand Coulee Dam, you look down on the great curtain of water that cascades over the face of the dam. From Memorial Day through Labor Day, 120 different combinations of colored lights play nightly on the water.

Loading onion seed

Harvesting winter wheat

Irrigating sugar beets

A FORMER DESERT, the Columbia Basin was one of the last parts of Washington to be settled. Wheat farmers didn't move in until around the turn of the century. The cattlemen came only a few years before them. Population was sparse. Ranchers had two, three, and four-thousand acre holdings, half of which lay fallow each year. Economic survival depended on rainfall and grain prices. Today on more than half a million acres irrigated by the hundreds of miles of canals south of Grand Coulee Dam, farmers grow almost seventy different crops—potatoes, sugar beets, alfalfa, corn, asparagus, peppermint, beans, apples, cherries—on more than 2,500 farm units of up to 160 acres each.

PHOTOGRAPHS BY TED SPIEGEL

GEORGE HUNTER

FARM NEAR GOLDEN is a friendly touch beneath rugged mountains that surround gentle valleys in the Big Bend region. North of here, in the 200-mile loop between Golden and Revelstoke, the river flows through a virtual wilderness.

FROM MOUNT REVELSTOKE you look down to the Columbia, a silvery thread twisting between spruce-covered slopes far below.

RAY ATKESON

THE INLAND EASTERN

EMPIRE AND OREGON

A vast lumbering, agricultural, and mining region spreads over the high plateau country of eastern Washington. It extends east across Idaho's Panhandle, north into British Columbia, and south into Oregon in a rich expanse of some 80,000 square miles that calls itself the "Inland Empire." Here is the historic Palouse country, which takes its name from the Indian tribe and is perhaps North America's richest wheatland, where huge combines crawl across tawny hillsides that reach as far as the eye can see. Here, too, are the sparkling lakes and rivers of Idaho's Panhandle; Spokane, Washington's second largest city; the agricultural centers of Walla Walla, Lewiston, and Moscow; Pendleton, in riding and roping rangeland in the shadow of Oregon's Blue Mountains. In eastern Oregon, the views are varied. Trails reach deep into the Blues, and the Wallowas to the east of the Blues, to crystal clear mountain lakes and streams where Eastern brook, rainbow, and golden trout are plentiful. On the Oregon-Idaho boundary, Hat Point overlooks the deepest part of the Snake River Gorge. Colorful hills rise above open rangeland dotted with juniper and sage; ancient fossil beds and lava formations tell a story of the past; and far down in the southeastern corner of the state, the lonely Owyhee River flows through spectacular rock-walled gorges and sagebrush country.

PHOTOGRAPH BY MARY RANDLETT

SCENIC HIGHLIGHTS in busy Spokane are restful Manito Park (above) and the tumultuous falls of the Spokane River (below). In addition to formal Duncan Gardens with its well-groomed topiary and precise flower beds, Manito Park has rose gardens, a Japanese garden, and a conservatory. Where the rushing waters of the Spokane River flow beneath Monroe Street Bridge, gondolas take viewers dramatically close to the torrent. The falls powered Spokane's first sawmill and flour mill. Now modern spillways supplement the original rapids in providing the city's electricity.

*OLD AND NEW contrast
in Spokane architecture. The
County Courthouse at left,
built in 1895, resembles an
elegant French chateau. A
relatively new addition to the
city scene, the Opera House,
below, built for Expo '74, serves
Spokane as a lively cultural
and convention center.*

PHOTOGRAPHS BY KEITH GUNNAR

A QUIET, SLEEPY RIVER meanders leisurely through the lake country of Idaho's Panhandle. The St. Joe originates in the Bitterroot watershed, where it is a rushing stream for its first fifty miles. In its placid lower reaches, its course takes it on a curving path between Lake Chatcolet and Round Lake (above), where a narrow fringe of tree-lined banks reflects in its still surface. Pend Oreille Lake (below) is the largest of the hundreds of sparkling, blue-green lakes in the Panhandle.

FOREST-RIMMED Lake Coeur d'Alene stretches north from Beauty Bay. The lakes and rivers of the Panhandle once were highways for prospectors, settlers, miners, and loggers, who followed the trappers and the missionaries. Lake Coeur d'Alene at one time floated more steam vessels than any other lake west of the Mississippi.

HARVEST TIME in the rich wheat fields of the Palouse brings forth an army of huge combines that crawl across the rolling hillsides, harvesting the tawny yield in one of the country's most productive wheat areas.

GRAIN STORAGE TOWERS loom up like city highrises from an otherwise unbroken expanse of wheat fields.

180   INLAND EMPIRE & EASTERN OREGON

A PATTERN TO FIT THE LAND is designed by this farmer as he guides his combine over a steep slope, following the contours of a golden field in the Skyrocket Hills of southeastern Washington.

181

HUGH PARADISE

HUGH PARADISE

TIDY LITTLE FARM near Lewiston is typical of those in Idaho's Palouse. From Grangeville to Lewiston, the highway goes through the Nez Perce Indian Reservation for much of the distance, and all along the way are reminders of Indian lore and of the days when pioneers trekked across Idaho's wilderness toward the Pacific shore.

ALONG THE WALLA WALLA RIVER the air is heavy with the scent of newly opened balsam poplar leaves in spring. The river begins in the Blue Mountains of Oregon and flows northwest through rich farmlands before joining the Columbia at Wallula, Washington.

INLAND EMPIRE & EASTERN OREGON 183

LOW-ROOFED CAVES at the base of steep basaltic cliffs once served as shelter and food-storage bins for Palouse Indians. Below the caves, the Palouse River cuts a deep canyon between cliffs on its way south to join the Snake. The Indians wove their own legends about the Palouse and believed that the mythological Big Beaver gouged out the canyon walls and the falls.

A ROARING CASCADE of muddy water fills the basin below Palouse Falls with clouds of mist at Palouse Falls State Park, where the Palouse River plunges 185 feet over a steep escarpment.

INLAND EMPIRE & EASTERN OREGON   **185**

EIGHT-SIDED BARN dominates the scene on a neat farm in the Wallowa Valley. The valley is horse country. Ranchers here raise high quality livestock, rodeo stock, and the Appaloosa horses developed by the Nez Perce Indians.

NEAR ELGIN a picturesque little church awaits the arrival of its congregation.

THE WALLOWA MOUNTAINS rise abruptly from the level fields of the Wallowa Valley in Oregon's northeastern corner. Popular Wallowa Lake, directly behind the low hill in the foreground, is only 4,400 feet high, at approximately valley elevation. The high center of the Wallowas is a land of rugged granite peaks, delightful alpine meadows, clear glacial lakes, and swift-flowing streams.

GILDEMEISTER

SNOW STILL BLANKETS the Elkhorn Range of the Blue Mountains in spring. The Anthony Lakes area (above) is ski country in the winter. In the summertime, its cool pine woods and quiet, parklike meadows attract vacationers from the hot, sunny valleys of northeastern Oregon.

WILLIAM APLIN

DAVID MUENCH

NO ROADS PENETRATE to the high lakes
of the Eagle Cap Wilderness. They are
reserved for the hiker and trail rider.
Within six square miles in Lake Basin, more
than thirty small lakes provide wilderness
camping spots and fishing in clear, cold
waters. The trail to Mirror Lake (above)
begins where the Lostine River road ends.

HAT POINT overlooks the deepest
part of the Snake River Gorge and
offers a view across the chasm to the
Seven Devils Mountains in Idaho.

THE JOHN DAY RIVER winds through fossil country in central Oregon. Ancient deposits trace Oregon's evolution through millions of years, yielding tiny patterned sea shells, perfect imprints of leaves of subtropical trees, and polished teeth and bones of camels, rhinoceroses, elephants, and oreodons. The oldest date back to the Cretaceous period, a time when an ancient sea covered almost all of Oregon.

THE CROOKED RIVER, true to its name, serpentines through a canyon far below the sheer cliffs, sculptures, balanced rocks, pinnacles, and spires that rise from flat lava plains at Smith Rock State Park.

190 INLAND EMPIRE & EASTERN OREGON

DAVID MUENCH

Yellow-headed blackbird

Great blue herons

Horned grebe

Trumpeter swans

Avocet

Common snipe

Canada geese

THE LONELY MARSHLANDS just south of Burns in eastern Oregon are almost deserted during the winter. Then, echoing down the skies, come the first cheery notes of migrating snow geese, and a mighty wave of migration begins again. During March and April, when thousands of birds are en route north along the Pacific flyway, great flights of snow geese, Canadian geese, whistling swans, pintail ducks, and other migrants stop at Malheur National Wildlife Refuge for food and rest. By early May most of the migrants have departed. The breeding birds remain to nest in the lakes, ponds, sloughs, swamps, and meadowlands of the refuge. Although birds are the main attraction, Malheur also supports deer, antelope, muskrats, mink, raccoons, and coyotes. A total of 248 species of birds and 51 species of mammals has been recorded.

PHOTOGRAPHS BY BUREAU OF SPORT FISHERIES AND WILDLIFE PHOTOGRAPHERS D. B. MARSHALL, E. KRIDLER, E. L. MCLAURY

Western grebe

Swainson's hawk

Snowy egret

Forster's tern

Black-necked stilt

Burrowing owls

Canada goose

LONELY BUILDINGS, many of them now-deserted remnants of a prosperous range heyday, stand alongside the Steens Mountain loop road in Oregon's dry southeastern corner.

194

HUNDREDS OF SHEEP *fill the Harper-Fields road when Basque herders and their dogs bring them down from the high pastures of Steens Mountain. The handful of ranches served by the road lie far back from it, mostly out of sight.*

LOOKING SOUTH *from Follyfarm, the Harper-Fields road stretches almost arrow-straight across dry lake beds at the eastern edge of Steens Mountain. Follyfarm is just a name now; the last building burned years ago.*

AN UNPEOPLED COUNTRYSIDE, softened by sagebrush and bunchgrass, and occasionally animated by cattle, jackrabbits, and antelope, stretches over Oregon's lonely southeastern corner. This is a country landscaped in lava. The massive Walls of Rome (above) are the vertical sides of a dry tributary of the Owyhee River, which slashes through rock-walled gorges and sagebrush country to the beginning of Owyhee Reservoir (below right). Near the Idaho Border, a lava flow dating back only five hundred years culminates at the Jordan Craters (above right), a large volcanic cone surrounded by several smaller ones.

HUGH PARADISE

HUGH PARADISE

EAST TO THE

ROCKIES

From the Palouse country on the west to the sharp spine of the Continental Divide, there stretches a splendid realm of scenic marvels. Mirrorlike lakes and tranquil mountain meadows are tucked among sky-piercing peaks. Sheep and cattle graze peacefully in quiet valleys. Wild rivers offer unforgettable experiences for river runners. There are streams to fish, mountains to climb, trails to ride. More than three million acres of pristine wilderness in central Idaho and western Montana have no road access but offer miles of trails for the hiker, the back packer, the horse or mule rider. Cupped in the 10,000-foot peaks of the Sawtooth Mountains is one of the country's most famous ski resorts. Not far from this mountain-walled world of rushing torrents and snowy splendor is the strange, stark lava landscape of Craters of the Moon National Monument. Along the spine of the Rocky Mountains, three national parks encompass some of the most beautiful mountain scenery in the world, and in between them are old mining towns, backwoods country, resort areas, and many reminders of the hardy pioneers who passed this way and of the Indians who traveled here before them.

PHOTOGRAPH BY FRANK JENSEN

MARTIN LITTON

UPRIVER FROM LEWISTON, the wild and rugged Snake forms a winding boundary between Oregon and Idaho. Sturdy little jet-propelled boats ride this turbulent waterway for some ninety miles. Sometimes the canyon sides slope away in great rolling hills; sometimes the rushing torrent has cut stratified layers into the lava walls. In Hells Canyon, the river enters the deepest chasm on the continent, where the Seven Devils Mountains reach to 9,393 feet above the east bank and Hat Point rises 6,982 feet on the Oregon side.

BIG BALDY LAKE is one of more than thirty little lakes tucked among the serrated peaks of the Seven Devils Mountains. The seven peaks, ranged in a semicircle, rise to heights of 9,000 feet and more.

FRANCES COLEBERD

MEADOW LAND like this ranch near New Meadows brought Basque sheepherders from the Pyrenees to this part of Oregon many years ago. Now Idaho has the largest Basque settlement in the United States.

ROBERT J. BROWN, JR.

EAST TO THE ROCKIES   201

GLACIAL LAKES and high alpine meadows reach far back into the Sawtooth Range at the edge of the Sawtooth Valley. At left, a motorboat heads up four-mile-long Redfish Lake toward Mount Heyburn.

DON NORMARK

BASQUE SHEEPHERDERS tend cattle and sheep in the meadows of the Sawtooth Range in summer. The traditional wagons are still in use, though they are no longer horse-drawn.

DON NORMARK

SERRATED PEAKS of the Sawtooth Range rise behind this tranquil scene in a wild hay meadow of the Sawtooth Valley.

DON NORMARK

TROUBLED WATERS of the Salmon's Middle Fork sweep between high canyon walls and challenge the skills of veteran rivermen. Organized float trips take adventurers through the pristine wilderness of the Idaho Primitive Area where the river falls about twenty feet per mile.

FROM BALDY'S SLOPES, skiers at Sun Valley look down on the rural mountain town of Ketchum and across to the soft contours of the snowy Sawtooths.

205

A LONE LIMBER PINE stands atop tumbled lava in Craters of the Moon National Monument. Though at first glance the land seems barren, closer examination reveals an abundance of animal and plant life.

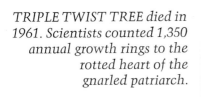

TRIPLE TWIST TREE died in 1961. Scientists counted 1,350 annual growth rings to the rotted heart of the gnarled patriarch.

206

DAVID MUENCH

AN ASTONISHING LANDSCAPE stretches as far as the eye can see. The expanse of lava fields, craters, and cinder cones at Craters of the Moon was left by a violent series of volcanic eruptions that ended more than 1,700 years ago.

207

FRANK JENSEN

OLD FAITHFUL (left) shoots a steaming fountain skyward for four or five minutes
almost hourly in Yellowstone National Park. It forms the most spectacular
clouds of steam in cool weather or early morning when the superheated water meets
cold air. The tumultuous Yellowstone River (above) begins in the high plateau
country just outside the park's southeast corner. At the head of the magnificent
Grand Canyon of the Yellowstone, it thunders from the top of a 308-foot cliff.

209

HIGH ABOVE TETON VILLAGE, this aerial tramway lifts sightseers in summer and skiers in winter up the eastern face of the Tetons to the summit of 10,446-foot Rendezvous Peak. It takes about ten minutes to make the 2.4-mile trip.

FROM THE TOP of Rendezvous Peak, you look into three Rocky Mountain states—Idaho, Montana, and Wyoming— and down on the steep slopes of the Jackson Hole ski area.

THE JAGGED TETONS rise straight
up from the sage-covered flats of
the Jackson Hole country. Although
the range extends for less than forty
miles, it contains some of the most
majestic mountain scenery in the
country. The peaks are in view from
almost every part of Grand Teton
National Park. They dominate the
skyline above the Snake River
(right and below), and 13,766-foot
Grand Teton, most majestic of
all the peaks in the range, looms
above sparkling Jenny Lake (left).

FRANK JENSEN

FRANK JENSEN

EARTHQUAKE LAKE filled a section of Madison Canyon in southwestern Montana when one of the strongest earthquakes in the history of the United States shook an eight-state area in 1959. As the earth shifted, half a mountain tumbled into Madison Canyon, blocking the Madison River and forming the new lake.

TRANQUIL CATTLE COUNTRY borders Yellowstone and Grand Teton national parks. Narrow, winding roads lead through ranch land where, as winter approaches, hay is stacked high in soft fields that are a sharp contrast to the jagged, awe-inspiring mountain scenery beyond.

SILENT AND DESERTED, the weathered buildings of Garnet, Montana, wait out the winter beneath a fluffy blanket of snow. When spring arrives, ghost town buffs once again will peer through paneless windows searching for reminders of Garnet's livelier gold mining days.

216

BIG HOLE BATTLEFIELD spreads across 360 acres in western Montana. The area is now a national monument, commemorating a battle fought in 1877 between U.S. troops and a band of Nez Perce Indians led by Chief Joseph.

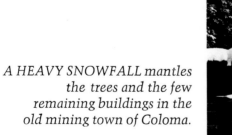

A HEAVY SNOWFALL mantles the trees and the few remaining buildings in the old mining town of Coloma.

Moose

Sparring elk

Hoary marmot

Black bear

Deer

Bighorn sheep

WILD ANIMAL SPECIES that would cause excitement elsewhere are commonplace sights in Glacier National Park. Moose are easy to see in large marshy areas, especially in the valley of the North Fork of the Flathead River. In high timbered valleys off the usual tourist paths, you find Rocky Mountain elk. In summer, deer are seen more often than elk, though there are actually few of them. There are two species: Rocky Mountain mule deer and Western white-tailed deer.
Large animals that you are not likely to see, although they inhabit the park, are cougars, Rocky Mountain wolves, and grizzly bears. Begging black bears are common along the main roads. The thrilling climbers of the park are the Rocky Mountain bighorns and the Montana mountain goats.

PHOTOGRAPHS BY DON WRIGHT

DON WRIGHT

*A SURE-FOOTED MOUNTAIN GOAT gambols over the rocks at Gunsight Pass,
easy to spot against the dark cliffs and the densely forested slopes that border
Gunsight Lake. The shaggy white animals often come within camera range.*

219

RAY ATKESON

ADJOINING GLACIER on the north is Canada's Waterton Lakes National Park. The two parks were combined in 1932 to form Waterton-Glacier International Peace Park, dedicated to the peace and friendship of the two nations. The imposing Prince of Wales Hotel is a picture-postcard sight at the foot of the upper Waterton Lake.

ST. MARY LAKE, longest lake in Glacier National Park, occupies a glacial trough bordered by magnificent peaks and knife-edged ridges. In 1910, when the park was established, it included about eighty glaciers; there are perhaps half as many today.

221

MALIGNE LAKE (above) mirrors the snow-crested peaks of the Queen Elizabeth Range. The boat trip to the end of the lake is one of the scenic highlights of Jasper National Park. Much-photographed Lake Louise (below) cupped in a vast amphitheater of towering, snowy peaks, is viewed across the gardens of Chateau Lake Louise.

WEDGE-SHAPED Mount Rundle looms above the Banff School of Fine Arts and Centre of Continuing Education. A Summer Festival here brings artists from all over the world.